DADVICE

50 Fatherly Life Lessons

By Dr. Jim Jobin

Dadvice 50 Fatherly Life Lessons
by Dr. Jim Jobin
Published by Kindle Direct Publishing

www.DadviceBook.com

ISBN: 9798642266571

Dedication

To my son James

It seems like it was only yesterday,
You were just a boy in the sun,
So quickly grew so tall,
You'd walk then run and fall.
It's funny how some things never change.

Soon you'll be a man and fully grown.
Stand to face the world all by yourself.
The others say they see,
That you're a lot like me.
It seems I gave you more than just my name.

It's hard to settle up for second best.
Son, winning alone is not the test.
You cannot see it now,
Someday you will somehow,
You're enough just the way you are.

Just keep your feet moving down the line.
The life you seek will come to you in time.
Remember who you are,
I'm never very far,
Dad is always with you in your heart.

Never mind the future or the plan,
I'm still your biggest fan,
Every day I think of you and you inspire me.
You are not a face within the crowd,
You've always made me proud.
You're twice the man that I could ever be.

To my daughter Juliana

Flying heart, tethered kite to string,
Hovers high so far, so near.
I listen as Juliana sings,
A song of whispers in my ear.

Loyal flame, heat and light my life,
Too cold without but burns within.
I'm wishing, for time itself to slow,
Frozen moments stacked end to end.

When you look to the stars,
In the dark of the night
I am there shining down
In the faintest of light
Though starlight may seem frail,
It's determined to last
As a beacon of hope
Reminding us of the past

Promises endure
forever yours, forever yours

Promises like pie crust,
A sweet but brittle frame.
Certain tears and countless fears,
Broken slices taste the same.
But know that I am with you,
My power and my strength,
As long as time endures.

Table of Contents

Preface

Everybody has a father, but not everybody has a *dad*.

A father is a guy who is biologically responsible for your existence. A dad is a guy who fills your life with paternal support, coaching, wisdom, and meaningful love.

As a psychotherapist I have seen hundreds of people who have a dad-shaped hole in their lives. It's so common that I often tease new fathers that their only job is to keep their kids out of my office.

I'm only half joking.

When I became a dad, more than a decade ago, I felt a tremendous burden to be useful to my kids. I had spent tens of thousands of hours as a clinical therapist carefully working through real people's lives, and I wanted to bring the best of that information to my children. I resolved to give them the most valuable insights I could, and, hopefully, to help them succeed in life.

That's how this book began. Over the course of 10 years I wrote down life lessons that emerged from my work as a therapist, hoping that, someday, it might be useful to my children or grandchildren. Over time it became a small library of notes written to be easily digestible, self-evident, and practical for real life. I had planned to just print the collection out and stash it in a box somewhere, until some fans of my podcast heard me read a passage of the book on-air and asked if they could have a copy. The more I shared it, the more people wanted it, and slowly, it dawned on me that these lessons are useful to everybody, everywhere.

My hope is that if you don't have a dad in your life, my words might fill a fraction of that void, and that if you do have a dad, you might imagine it's him saying these things in his own way. As a franchise, dads across the world generally consent to you giving us credit for smart things other people say, so I'm sure he's fine with it.

You should know that this book isn't designed to be read in a straight line, so feel free to hop around as you see topics that interest you. However, I ask that you don't read the epilogue of the book until you have read all the other chapters. I have a message for you that I want to make sure you understand, and I don't think it will make sense unless you've heard me throughout the book.

Someone once said, "A father is more than a hundred school masters." That person was obviously a dad, because that statement was very wise. We dads have a unique way of teaching, which has a flavor of humor, impatience, and sincerity.

I hope you enjoy encountering my personal style of dadvice in this book, and I hope that it becomes a useful reference in your life going forward.

Thanks for reading.

Love,

Dad

Work for it

Like most kids, you wanted toys. Like most parents, I avoided the toy aisle like jury duty.

But inevitably, you'd find your way there and start playing with things. As I announced it was time to leave, you'd make your case for whatever toy had caught your eye that day: why I should buy it for you, and what you would do with it.

For a long time, I bought you toys and didn't think much about it. Until one day, I went into your room and saw all those toys laying around—unplayed-with and uncared-for—while you complained that you were bored and needed me to entertain you.

When next we were at the store, you came upon something you *really* wanted. This time I told you how much it cost, and offered to let you earn the money to buy the toy. This approach seemed novel, so you stupidly agreed to my scam, and in doing so, lost forever the innocent ignorance of not knowing how capitalism works.

Chores. You did them.

You earned a pittance with each one and dreaded the ever-growing list of them each day. You kept that toy in your mind the whole time and beamed with pride as you bought and paid for it yourself at the store.

For weeks you never put that toy down. It seemed there was no limit to the things you could do with it. You'd step over more expensive and more interesting toys as you endlessly enjoyed the one you had bought. You were careful not to lose it. You always kept it clean. You played the crap out of that thing.

Somebody once said, "That which is too easily obtained is too lightly esteemed." That means you will value the things you've worked for, and won't the things you didn't.

So don't despise the effort you gave to have what you've got. Be proud of your stuff and your lifestyle, and don't envy those who got what they have easily.

You've earned it.

Bury the noise

The half-life of sound is 1 millisecond.

This means that if you snap your fingers, by the time you've heard the sound, it has been out of existence three lifetimes longer than it lived.

Despite how fleeting sound is, you might be replaying the words of others over and over in your mind, allowing ancient sounds—which existed, in reality, only briefly—to haunt you and change the way you live your life.

That's normal, but consider this carefully: words only have power if you memorialize them.

There are people in your past whose words are nothing but hurtful, false, and meaningless noise, which, if believed, can become a prison of pain for your mind. A prison that's locked from the inside.

We give such words power by keeping their memory alive, by holding onto them though they died long ago.

Bury them. They don't exist anymore.

Don't look down

Once there was this movie in which government agents had special red-light flashing pens that could delete people's memories. They used the devices to make sure the world didn't find out about the existence of aliens.

I remember thinking that if the truth came out, humanity would be way more excited about the memory-eraser-thing than about the aliens. Who wouldn't want to be free of the worst moments of their past? I could care less if space-faring, octopus-like creatures are abducting farmers in New Mexico; give me that blinky, nightmare-destroying pen thing!

One of the funny quirks of our memories is that they haunt us. We remember where we've been, those lowest points, and it frightens us. Sometimes we flash back to those places when we are, actually, the furthest from them that we could possibly be; but that distance doesn't save us from the shrill of terror that floods in from the past.

When you were little we used to go to the park, and you played a game called *Climb Up on Something*

High Enough to Give Dad a Panic Attack. You were good at that game.

But one time, when you were climbing up an especially high (for your age) spiral, metal thing, you were doing great until you neared the top and looked down at your feet to adjust yourself. You froze. Suddenly you went from a devil-may-care high-wire acrobat to a terrified statue. Looking back to where you started gave you two thoughts simultaneously: "Wow, that's a long way down," and, "I will hit that ground in a microsecond if I slip."

Of course, the remedy for your fear wasn't to tell you that gravity doesn't exist, or to promise that I'd catch you if the worst happened. I didn't try to convince you that there was no danger.

Instead I told you to ignore it. To not look at it. Sure, it's there, but it's not useful to see that. Ironically, you aren't made safer by increasing your awareness of danger. You're made safer by continuing the climb.

Looking down from our high points or looking back at our worst memories can paralyze us with fear. Sometimes the best strategy is to simply not look at it and instead focus on what's ahead of us.

If nothing changes, nothing changes

When I was a kid, my mom used to tell me to make my bed. Every morning she'd ask if I had done it before we left for school. I'd say, "Yes." We'd leave.

When we got home, I'd be in trouble. She would show me my bed with covers haphazardly pulled up over the pillows, everything untucked and wrinkled and accuse me of lying to her that morning. I'd protest that I'd done what she asked, but she wasn't having it. The bed wasn't made.

This went on for a few weeks almost daily: yelling and tears, pillows and blankets, confusion and anger. She couldn't understand how I didn't manage to make my bed. It seemed to her that I was either an idiot or a pathological liar.

One day, I got home from school, and I came into my room to see my mother sitting on my bed, crying. I felt terrible that I had failed her yet again, and even more awful that she took it so personally. I sat beside her, preparing myself for her scorn and feeling hopeless to ever solve the problem; but then, she did something completely unexpected.

She apologized. She said that, all this time, she couldn't understand how I wouldn't make my bed as she'd asked, until it dawned on her that she had never taught me how to make a bed. I was 10 years old; I knew what a made bed looked like after Mom was done with it, but nobody had ever showed me how. It never occurred to me to ask, and it never occurred to her to teach me.

Mom calmly showed me how to pull down the sheets and blankets, fold them beneath the mattress, and line everything up neatly. She showed me how to stack my pillows in the right order and then smooth everything with my palm. It was simple now that I knew how.

In life, we sometimes feel like we are going crazy, facing a situation, problem, or pattern that we can't solve. We are able to identify what's not working, we are able to identify the outcome we want, and we are willing to get that outcome, yet no matter how hard we try, it never seems to come together. Sometimes, to summarize Albert Einstein, *we are insanely doing the same thing over and over, yet expecting different results.*

Be willing to experiment with how you are tackling your problems. Try new approaches and be open-minded to fresh ideas. If you want changed outcomes, you have to change your process.

Presume innocence

Growing up, I enjoyed watching cartoons about superheroes who had amazing powers. One of my favorites was a show called *X-Men,* which was about a group of mutants who evolved to have abilities like laser eyes, claw hands, or control over the weather.

My favorite X-man was their leader, Professor Charles Xavier, "Professor X" for short. He had the ability to read people's minds. That doesn't seem as exciting as making the sky spit out tornadoes, but danged if it wasn't the most useful ability of all.

It seemed that all the X-Men did was fight. They'd fight bad guys, governments, good guys, sometimes one another—they had these incredible powers, but all it did was make them afraid of what the others might do.

Not Professor X, though. He didn't have to wonder what people would do. He knew what everybody was thinking. It made some of the stories really interesting, because he realized that even the bad guys often had good intentions. Professor X was the only character who lived fearlessly, because he didn't assume the worst in others, and he didn't worry about what people might do.

You and I can't read people's minds—well, you can't. And I know what you're thinking (do you see what I did there?): how can we know the intentions of other people if we can't hear their thoughts?

The simple answer is that we can't. We can't know if our coworker is out to get us, or if our spouse stubbornly refuses to acknowledge our contributions, or if our dad wrote this book in a desperate grab at fame. If we assume the worst, it will cause us to think, feel, and even behave differently toward others. It will make us suspicious, afraid, and sad.

But Professor X and I generally find that people aren't malicious. The best explanation for why they do what they do is usually the one with innocent intentions.

Your co-worker just wants to shine at work; your spouse is distracted but appreciates you; and your dad wrote this book because he loves money—I mean, *you.*

The American legal system requires that anybody who is facing scrutiny should be presumed innocent, and that guilt carries the burden of proof beyond a shadow of a doubt. That is a good principle to live by.

When you interact with the people in your life, presume that their actions, words, and thoughts are innocent. They aren't out to get you. They don't want you to suffer. *Most* people are just passively meandering through life, trying their best, and not going out of their way to cause problems.

Giving others the benefit of the doubt will make you fearless and calm. It will help you avoid behaving unkindly, and it will free you from the fear, anger and sadness that comes with believing the worst about people.

Don't just do something, stand there

When I was in college, I was friends with a couple who had just announced that they were pregnant. Our whole group was thrilled for them, and it was all any of us could talk about for weeks—until the day my phone rang.

When I answered, I heard the husband on the line sobbing, unable to speak. As I listened, I heard his wife's voice in the background, shrill and full of fear. Finally, my friend stammered out a single word that landed on me like an anvil: miscarriage.

I quickly called our other friends, and we planned to meet at the couple's home to comfort them when they returned. As their car pulled up, I saw the couple's faces, ashen and expressionless. They were engulfed in pain, and it took everything they had to walk into the house and sit on the couch in silence.

Immediately our well-meaning friends attempted to console the couple. They said things like, "This is just God's plan," and, "One day you will forget all about this." The words twisted like knives in the wounds of the couple, who could do little more than sit lifelessly and take it.

Friends offered to call the couple's family and explain what had happened, and some even started vaguely sharing the news on social media. It was a frenzy of energy that tormented the couple until, finally, they asked everybody to leave.

When we see somebody who is in pain, it is only natural to want to attend to them. But when real tragedy is happening, any attempt we make to "help" a person almost always hurts them. It makes us uncomfortable to see somebody else unhappy, and so we deny them their sadness and insist that they feel better. But platitudes are painful, and soothing another's sorrow is selfish.

The kindest thing you can offer to a grieving person is silence. Stand in their presence and witness their suffering; allow yourself to feel their pain and remain in the mess without trying to clean it up.

Imagine grief as a black smoke filling the room. By breathing it in, you're leaving a little less for the hurting to inhale. You can't spare them the noxious fumes of sadness, but you can absorb it for them.

The kindest thing you can do in the presence of unbearable pain is to bear it.

None of us is our worst moment

I think a lot about how different humans are from the rest of the animal kingdom. We can dream and plan for the future. We can sacrifice ourselves for ideas. I think we are also the only species that collects stamps.

Another thing that is peculiar to our conscious mind is regret. We remember a thing we said or did and feel haunted by it. The memory stabs at us and tells us that we are horrible.

Regret looms like an executioner's axe in our memories. Those feelings can become intrusive and interrupt our lives, telling us that we are villains, fools, or unworthy of joy.

The thing about being conscious is that we are too complex to be guided by instinct alone. We learn by doing, by feeling, by error. We bumble and crash through life, getting the hang of things as we go. We make mistakes, and we learn from them.

But in the ocean of a human being, a mistake is only a speck of sand. A moment, an hour, a day, is nothing in the long, winding story of a human life. Our regrets try to tell us who we are, but at best, they tell us only what once happened.

We have all made mistakes. Those mistakes hurt to think about, but that hurt reveals our true character. Clearly, if those memories bother us, it means that whatever happened is incongruent with who we really are.

Do not allow yourself to be tricked into thinking you are your worst moments. You are ever-changing, ever-growing, and infinitely complex. You are a galaxy of ideas and choices and thoughts.

You are more than a moment.

Salt the jar

When you were a kid, I sometimes took you on hikes out in nature. Usually, along the way, the path would become unclear. Do we turn here between these two bushes or squeeze through those rocks?

The answer would be revealed through our detective work. What did other people do? If we saw footprints, broken branches, or tamped down grass, we had our answer about where the path continued. We'd sigh in relief and go on our way.

Knowing what other people selected gave us the idea that one path had more value than another. It is a shortcut in human reasoning that allows us to make assumptions and choices, and it doesn't just influence where we hike.

If a person appears to be valued by other people we tend to value them too. This is why, in your own life, it is important that you teach people how to treat you.

What you wear, the people you surround yourself with, and what you have accomplished are all important clues which communicate value. If you don't reveal these clues, then other people won't benefit from them, and neither will you. I know you're not comfortable showing off, and I know you prefer action to words. But learning the skill of signaling your value to other people is vital to your future success.

When you next go to a coffee shop, notice the tip jar on the counter. Is it empty? Probably not. Even if you're the first customer to walk in that morning, the tip jar will already have money in it. The staff put it in there; it's called "salting the jar". They do that to give you the impression that other customers gave them a tip, and so maybe you should too.

This is what I want you to do in your life. Allow others to get the impression that you are a valuable person, that they should treat you with respect, that you have something to offer the world. Because you are, they should, and you do.

Remember: teach others to value you or they won't.

Don't poo poo
where you yum yum

When I think of the greatest hero in history I don't think of an athlete, an actor, or even a world leader.

I think of a man who saved more lives than any doctor who has ever lived. A man who single-handedly lifted civilization from the sewers into the sky. The wizard of waste management, the godfather of gooey pooey, English sanitation engineer John Snow.

Snow's great achievement was realizing that poop makes people sick. For hundreds of years, humans died merely because we didn't know how to make our dookie go away. We scattered it on the streets or in our drinking water, while having no clue that it was poisoning us the whole time.

John Snow saved us all just by telling us to separate our bathroom from our kitchen.

But what you may not realize is that unsanitary waste has many forms. The crap we say can be just as toxic as the crap we don't.

Similarly, bringing your love life into your work life is not in your best interest.

Complaining to your co-workers about your boss is not in your best interest.

Talking politics, religion, or sharing your deeply held personal beliefs during meetings is not in your best interest.

Whatever kind of crap you're relieving yourself of, it doesn't belong in the same place where you make your money.

Protect your financial health by keeping it free of anything negative that comes out of you.

Don't buy milk
at the hardware store

There are something like 8 billion humans currently existing on this ball of mud we call Earth.

As you live your life, you're going to have to interact with quite a few of those people. Over time, you will find that there are lots of different types of them.

This is important. Even though human beings have a lot in common, we are not all the same, and you shouldn't have the same expectations for everybody you meet.

There are people from whom you will seek love, but who won't be capable of loving you in a nourishing way.

There are people from whom you would like to receive understanding, but who just can't understand.

There are people who you will wish treated you with respect, but who continuously won't.

On the one hand, I want you to believe that all humans are capable of change. On the other, I want you to understand the folly of going to a hardware store to buy milk.

They don't have it. There is no point in getting angry and yelling at the cashier. They are just as confused as you are.

Go get what you need from those that have it.

Stay out of crab buckets

I grew up in the desert, so I don't know much about the ocean.

One time, on vacation in California, I was walking on a pier and saw a man pulling up a rope from the water. Attached to the rope was a basket with crabs inside of it. When he got his catch up to the pier, I watched as he opened the trap and shook the crabs out into a large bucket. Then he turned and threw the basket back into the sea.

The crab bucket was nearly overflowing with the wily ninja-water-spiders, their clamping claws and kicking legs a scramble as the crabs struggled to escape. I figured the man would place a lid or net on top of the bucket to keep his bounty from escaping.

He didn't.

For, like, 10 minutes, I just stared, waiting for a crab to slide off the top of the stack, flop onto the wooden deck, and make a break for it. But it never happened. They squirmed and fought, but they never left the bucket. Finally, I asked the guy what he was using to keep the crabs from escaping.

He explained that he didn't have to do anything. The crabs stop each other from escaping. Each time one of them tries to leave the bucket, the rest reach up and grab him and keep him in.

To demonstrate, the man picked up two crabs and tossed them into an empty bucket together. As soon as one crab began making its way out of the bucket, the other would clamp onto the first's legs and yank it back down. The process would repeat, over and over again, no matter which crab was trying to escape.

He explained that one crab in a bucket will escape, but that two will hold each other down until they hit the dinner plate.

In life, you are going to meet *crabs*: people who don't lift you up but instead pull you down, people who can't stand seeing you succeed and will sabotage you whenever possible.

You can't negotiate with them. You can't compromise with them. They are crabs.

So do your best to stay out of crab buckets, away from people who bring you down and stand in the way. Also remember that if you end up in a crab bucket, it's probably because you, too, are a crab, just as vicious and self-interested as the rest of them.

Be encouraging to others, be genuine, and desire the success of the team as much as your own.

To stay out of crab buckets, don't be a crab.

Don't stuff your happiness

We spend most of our lives avoiding sadness and convincing ourselves that something or someone can make us feel better.

This search influences pretty much everything we do. It's why we fall in love. It's why we have children. It's why we get jobs and build cities and vote.

The Declaration of Independence even says that the "pursuit of happiness" is so important that it is a human right on par with life and freedom. Though the founders believed that life and liberty were things we could *have*, they believed that happiness was something we could only *pursue*.

They weren't wrong.

Accepting that simple fact is the beginning of wisdom. Most humans will spend their whole lives trying to buy things or experiences to make themselves happy.

But stuff won't make you happy.

The marketing people will tell you that whiter teeth, colder drinks, or shinier shoes will make you happy. The reality is that happiness is a fleeting moment of satisfaction and was never intended to last.

You can pursue it, but you can't buy it.

Float like a duck

When I was kid my grandparents took me on a trip through the western U.S. We saw the Grand Canyon, hiked Zion National Park, and hit the buffets in Las Vegas; but the one thing I remember from that entire trip was a boat ride on Lake Powell.

It was ferociously windy that day. Even though we were on one of those large sight-seeing boats, the choppy waves rocked us and the gusts nearly blew me off the deck. My grandmother had to clutch the neck of my shirt with a kung-foo hold to keep me from lifting off like a kite. I could barely hear my grandfather's voice through the whir of air as he called out, "Look, a duck!"

Normally ducks aren't exciting, but this one stood out. His green head and brown body gliding atop the roiling lake while sprays of water shouted over him from wind sheared waves. The little hollow-boned bird seemed unbothered by the elements. He almost seemed bored.

My grandfather saw my confusion and leaned down to explain the apparent contradiction to me. He pointed just below the creature and told me to look carefully at his feet. At first it seemed the duck *had* no feet in the clear water, until my eyes caught up to the blur of orange wildly sweeping in every direction beneath the animal.

The duck's legs were a frenzy, fighting the lake and the wind with every ounce of his strength. Above the surface he was serene; beneath it his efforts were olympic.

That duck reminds me of being a parent.

The reason my grandparents took me on that trip was because my parents were selling off their belongings and preparing to be evicted from their home. They had lost everything and when I returned we were homeless, a family of four living in a friend's 100 square foot basement.

Looking back I can't imagine how hard it must have been for them, though at the time I had no clue. On the surface my parents appeared calm, they concealed the incredible effort they made to keep our family afloat in the tempest of hard times. They gave me the gift of ignorance so my childhood could be peaceful.

I've tried to give that gift to you as well. There is a lot you don't know about what I have gone through to keep you safe and bored. There have been times in my life that I've felt just like that duck appearing to float lazily while invisibly fighting to survive.

Floating like a duck is an act of love. My parents appeared calm for my benefit and I've tried to do the same for you. I hope you will also do this for the people you love: fighting for them every day with all the strength you have, but concealing your rigor for their benefit.

I don't want you to hold everything in. I don't want you to sacrifice without a sound. I do however want you to appreciate the power of grace under pressure and the sense of safety your serenity may give to others.

The dignity of risk

I've long struggled with feeling responsible for other people, most of all you. It's caused me to spend a lot of energy trying to baby-proof the world to protect you. For a time, I guess that was the right thing to do.

But eventually, I had to realize that if I protected you from reality and shielded you from harm, I was, in essence, robbing you of your freedom. If you can't suffer, or hurt, or fail, then how can you be the master of your own life?

I decided that I owed you the respect to live with risk. Though I'd cringe watching you live that out, I came, in time, to see that it made you a better person. It made you real.

I've learned that humans, for the most part, will figure it out. Trying to limit their ability to fail in many ways deprives them of the inherent dignity of choice and consequence.

In your life, be careful not to rob others of their dignity by removing all the risk. I know you care, and

I know you don't want anybody to fail, but don't let your love stop another person from growing.

Play the tape forward

Not everything in life is predictable. The lottery, for example. Or the Cubs in October.

But a lot of things are predictable, and you can usually anticipate the outcomes with a pretty good degree of certainty, if you think about them.

When you were a kid, I used to playfully try to teach you this when you screwed something up, which, as I recall, you didn't find very funny at the time.

For example, you'd throw the ball around inside the house despite my objections and would knock a lamp off a table. When you turned toward me in shock and fear, I'd stoically ask, "What have you learned?"

When I first started that bit you'd give me a real answer, like, "Don't play ball inside the house." When you got older you'd just mumble, "Nothin'," and get started cleaning up the broken pieces of the lamp.

I found you more charming when you were younger.

But as patronizingly simple as my question was, I hoped you'd figure out the lesson. If you anticipate consequences, you can avoid a lot of brokenness and misery in life.

Think through your actions before you do them. Play the choice forward and imagine what might go wrong or what possible outcomes there might be. Then make a decision.

No pressure, no diamonds

The best papers I ever wrote in school were started the day before they were due. I know I told you to get started early and not wait until the last minute, but this is one of those "do as I say, not as I do" sort of things.

Anyway, I've noticed that the whole last-minute phenomenon shows up in more than just writing. There is something that turns on inside people when they are under the gun. Something is revealed inside of them that explodes to life under incredible stress.

I'm not sure if you knew this, but diamonds are made of coal. The pretty, expensive, shimmering, expensive, rare, and expensively expensive rocks that countless people are scammed into gluing onto jewelry are made from exactly the same thing as coal.

Coal is that stuff you buy in bags from the grocery store, which has so little value that we literally set it on fire to make hot dogs warm. Also, Santa puts it in your stocking if you don't wash Dad's car every weekend.

A diamond is just smooshed coal. There is no actual difference, except that one has been put under a crap-ton of pressure and the other hasn't.

People are like that too.

When you are stressed out and overloaded, I need you to remember that what you are experiencing is actually changing you into something precious, durable, and valuable.

All people are made of the same stuff, but the smooshed ones become diamonds.

Race the ghost car

I am old enough to remember a time before the internet, but also young enough to have participated in and been affected by it daily.

Before we had social media to boast about our smallest accomplishments (going to the gym, making our own lunch, getting a haircut), we pretty much lived our lives without recognition. People would find out via Christmas card photos who had a new child or a new spouse, and we didn't have the ability to post a snarky comment in response.

We didn't compare ourselves to others as much. We didn't know what our friends from high school ate for dinner. We had only ourselves to think about.

It reminds me of a racecar video game I used to play; it had a mode called "time trial". In this mode, you didn't race other cars, you raced the clock. To assist you with this, the game provided a transparent "ghost car" to race alongside you. It was the past version of yourself, there only to give perspective on your progress; it couldn't affect you in any way.

Interestingly, the best times I ever got in that video game were when I was racing that ghost car, not when I was racing others. To be the best version of myself, I needed to compare only to the last version of myself. Other cars only distracted me from my race.

In life, you are going to feel compelled to compare yourself to everybody else, but I warn you that this just slows you down. Look to your own goals, and gauge your progress by your own growth.

You'll be happier and winning is an illusion anyway.

Live meaningfully

Your grandfather had a saying about painting that has always stuck with me: "This is the secret to happiness: if you enjoy painting, maintain a lifestyle befitting the income of a painter."

Basically, "Live within your means."

I realize that seems dry and uninteresting, certainly not as exciting as a credit-card vacation or an extra 1,000 square feet in a house. But it actually allows a lot of other interesting things to happen.

Somebody once said, "Be not made a beggar by banqueting upon borrowing." If you are worried about a mortgage or credit card bills, you won't look at your job as something you enjoy. You will look at it as a prison, a place you are forced into because of your past choices.

Believe me when I tell you that avoiding a luxurious lifestyle so that you can enjoy what you do with your career is an extremely meaningful choice.

For now ain't forever

When you were little, you were obsessed with growing up.

You'd tell me all the things you couldn't wait to do and were super impatient, constantly wishing for time to speed up so that you could be big. You'd complain about how long it was taking, and for you, it really was going by slowly. To grow from 5 to 10 years old was literally an entire lifetime.

But to me, you grew up instantly. One moment you were clutching my legs as I stomped around the living room. The next you were off living your life without me.

It happened so fast. Too fast.

I know you are eager for what's ahead, and you should be. But don't forget to appreciate what's right in front of you, to enjoy the age and the stage you are in right now.

I feel like, my entire life, I've heard myself say that I don't have time. No time to go for a walk. No time to play catch in the yard. No time to have dinner with the family.

Then one day, a person on the other side of the world coughed, and a global pandemic began. It resulted in the world stopping—no jobs to go to, no business to do. I worked from home for months and experienced an abundance of empty time.

As scary as that was for me, I also came to appreciate how important it is to make time for the people in my life, to create empty voids of nothing on purpose, so that I can toss a ball in the backyard or roast a marshmallow with my children.

The most valuable moments of my life won't be the blurs of busyness but the still, uneventful pools of time where I enjoyed what was around me. I hope you will make it a habit to enjoy your time rather than rushing through it.

On the other hand, I also know that sometimes life can grow stagnant, and waiting for change can be painful. I've spent plenty of nights longing for my life to move forward, wondering if it ever would.

The Bible reminds us that "this too shall pass". No matter how bad things get, no matter how challenging a moment is, the truth is that nothing is eternal. Your life *will* change, that fact should give you gratitude in the good times and hope in the bad times.

Mind the blade

When I was 10 years old, my Dad bought me a knife.

It wasn't like a machete or anything, just a tiny black Swiss Army knife. But I remember, when he gave it to me, I had a sense of awe and wonder looking at it. It was a real weapon.

I opened it hastily and immediately started whipping it around, making *whoosh* noises like I'd seen in cartoons. My Dad wisely grabbed my arm mid-whoosh and gripped me tightly.

He warned me that the knife was not a toy, and that I had to be responsible when I had it opened, and that I could Burt myself or might Burt somebody else I don't remember I stopped listening because I was imagining throwing the knife at the tree I saw outside the window.

Later that night, I woke up and spirited my knife into my closet. In the glow of a flashlight, I opened and admired the shining piece of sharp metal as I dragged it against the fingerprints of my thumb. I needed to *use* the thing. Cut something. So I pulled out a new G.I. Joe action figure still in its package and began sawing away at the cardboard to free the soldier from the plastic.

I slipped.

Had I listened to Dad's speech about Burt, I would have learned that you always cut *away* with a knife, never toward yourself. A small, yet invaluable piece of information, it turned out, as I cradled my bleeding hand in the dark closet that night.

I was gripped with fear and panic. This weapon had hurt me. I had hurt me. It happened so quickly. Was I going to die? Should I go get help? Would I get in trouble? What if they take away my shiny black knife? The world was complicated, and I was bleeding.

In the many years and many knives since this incident, I have never once cut myself again. I am careful now, a perspective I have shouted at you many times as you transported scissors from one side of a room to another, and especially the first time I gave you a knife.

Of course, this mindfulness extends to more than just sharp things, it applies to anything that you ought to show respect for and take seriously. In life, you will have access to an infinity of means to destroy or harm yourself. Imagine this is me snagging your arm in the air, mid-whoosh; but, really, listen to me for a second.

The moment you fail to respect the destructive power of this thing, it will harm you. You can hold it. You can use it. But at all times, you must be aware of it. Know what it is, and wield it skillfully. Remember that this thing doesn't *want* to harm you, but it will if you handle it poorly, if you think of it as a toy, when in reality it is a tool.

If you aren't careful you could *hurt* (not Burt) yourself or somebody else. You're old enough to possess this thing, but you must never become too comfortable with it. Your mind must always be on it.

Bet on horses

Close your eyes and imagine you hear the clopping of hooves outside your window.

Clip, clop, clip, clop, clip, clop.

Now, without looking through your imaginary window, tell me what animal is making that noise.

Did you guess "zebra"? No? Good. That's because you're not an idiot.

In life, we often face situations where multiple interpretations might be correct. We may jump to conclusions that are unusual and terrifying, and seeing things in this way can lead us to make big decisions with bad consequences.

So when we aren't sure what the best explanation is—just like when we aren't sure what's making that clip-clop sound outside—we should probably think of horse-type explanations, and not of zebras.

Zebras are rare. Exotic. Unusual. They definitely exist, and there is a non-zero chance that one is walking outside your window. But it's not the best explanation.

Horses are common. Boring. Ordinary. I promise that, wherever you live right now, there is a horse within 20 miles of you. For my money, that's a horse outside your window.

Next time you find yourself freaking out or feeling depressed, ask yourself whether you are imagining a rare and exciting zebra possibility or a common and ordinary horse one. Even if you can't rule out a zebra, you'd still be better off assuming it isn't one.

Bet on the horse.

Get naked

People tend to cover up.

They layer themselves in personalities and behaviors, so that we won't see their insecurities.

Sometimes they try to seem intimidating, powerful, confident, funny, disengaged, carefree, or distracted; but all of that is just shiny armor to protect their soft skin.

In reality, they are hyperaware of their weaknesses and are terrified other people will find out. They pretend to be strong, but they actually aren't.

In contrast, naked people are intimidating.

Sure, there's that "maybe they're crazy" aspect of things, but also it's strange that they seem so unaffected by the opinions of others.

It's not that they "don't care"; in fact, they probably do. It's that they are beyond caring. They are so comfortable with themselves that it makes others uncomfortable.

I've spent years trying to use humor or confidence to mask my own insecurities. I've bragged or put others down in the hope that somehow I might protect myself from being discovered as a fragile and brittle human being.

But what I've found is that, when I have allowed myself to be vulnerable—discarded the cover-up and basked in the luminescent, milky whiteness of my flabby, untanned personality—people don't attack.

They see my lack of armor, and, instead of pouncing on me, they tend to be stunned and almost intimidated. They admire my power.

I know there are things you don't like about yourself, things that other people have used to make you feel self-conscious or to wound you. But ironically, if you want to be powerful and fearless, you may have to be vulnerable and transparent.

To get power, get naked.

Metaphorically, though. There are still laws against indecent exposure, and I prefer that you wear clothes.

Suggest your solutions

When you're facing a problem, and you aren't sure what to do, imagine that your dumbest friend just called you with the same problem.

Now pretend to give that friend advice on what they should do. Calm them down. Help them understand the misguided ways they are seeing the situation, and then tell them what's really happening.

Offer them some ideas of how they can make matters slightly better. Keep them focused on what's happening right now, not what *could* happen way down the road.

As you speak, listen to yourself. Realize that you are actually a very good advisor. Appreciate the way you would see everything differently if you were helping a friend with their problem rather than facing your own.

Use that method when you feel afraid, overwhelmed, or uncertain. You'll be surprised how much wisdom you have to offer yourself.

Give people flowers
while they can smell them

Graveyards are quiet places.

Most people don't enjoy them, and neither do I, but I've always appreciated what they bring out in us. A graveyard is where people confess how they felt about somebody they admired.

"Eulogy" literally means "good words". But ironically, we speak these words in the silence of the graveyard, where the person who would have most enjoyed hearing them cannot. We lay wreaths of flowers on the casket of a person who can't smell them.

One of the biggest regrets people have in life is when it's too late to tell somebody how they felt about them, after they've gone their separate ways or have left the living altogether.

Don't wait to tell people how you feel. Make it a habit. Write them a note, leave them a message, pull them aside and tell them what you enjoy about them, for no other reason than that they are able to hear it.

Navigation before acceleration

I remember going on the freeway for the first time when I was learning how to drive.

65 MPH was terrifying; it was twice as fast as I'd ever gone in my life. I clutched the wheel, locked my arms, held my breath, and cursed anybody who honked for me to go faster.

Then my instructor made me accelerate to 75!

I was sure the blurred colors outside my window were the last thing I'd see before my car ripped through space-time and burst into a new dimension. The minutes ticked like hours, each mile earned through dry eyes and wet palms.

After nearly half an hour on the highway, my teacher mercifully directed me to take the next exit.

What happened next is something I'll never forget.

I turned onto the ramp and rolled along as it bent and sloped in parallel with a quiet suburban street. The serene 35 MPH sign greeted me as I joined traffic and glided through an intersection. Finally, I could relax. The rollercoaster ride was over, and I was back to what I knew. As my heart stopped pounding in my chest my instructor's words caught me off guard.

"Slow down."

I thought he must have lost his mind. Speed is *bad*. Slow is *good*. I was glad to be off the freeway and coasting along gently on a typical easy road. Why go any slower? But as I looked down at the speedometer, I was shocked to see I was still going 75 MPH!

I eased the brake and halved my speed; it felt as if the whole world were suddenly standing still. The landscape on the side of the road crawled, and I found myself watching time go by in slow motion.

Velocitation. That's what my instructor called it. My mind had gotten used to the faster speed, so I'd adapted, changed. My brain moved quicker to survive the freeway. Fast was my new normal, and what used to be normal now felt slow. It took a while to recalibrate myself, so that driving on the city streets didn't feel like slogging through mud.

The same experience is often had in life. You may find yourself in a new job or in a new relationship that is much more than you're used to. The speed or success is terrifying as you navigate wildly with shaking hands and clenched teeth.

But even those living in the fast lane eventually exit.

When you do, regular life will feel boring, sad, or disappointing. You'll feel unsatisfied and underwhelmed.

Velocitation is a trick of the mind. In time, you'll recalibrate and realize that the speed at which your life moves has nothing to do with your happiness or success.

Blinding speed gives us a rush, and slowing down can feel mundane, but speed doesn't matter if you have no direction.

If you are going at light speed in the wrong direction, there is no progress. On the other hand, if you move at a snail's pace in the right direction, you are ahead.

Somebody once said, "We all want progress, but progress means getting nearer to the place where you want to be. If you are on the wrong road, progress means doing a U-turn."

In life, I expect that you will try multiple directions as you find your way. At some point, you may even speed up and become used to a certain way of living, and if you depart from that path, you'll feel frustrated with how slow life may become. But remember that where you are going is more important than how quickly you get there.

Embrace mystery

I spent a lot of my life trying to prove things I believed in: religion, politics, science.

I would do lots of research, form an opinion, get so far into the debate that the people in my life had no idea what I was talking about. I'd look down on everybody with a self-assured, invulnerable confidence.

I was right.

I had it all figured out.

I had an answer to everything.

I was so unhappy.

See, the surer I was about things, the lonelier I became. I pushed people away with my hot words and foaming mouth. I discovered that having all the answers had little value if nobody wanted to talk about them with me.

At some point, I started appreciating mystery. I began suspecting that maybe the best questions don't have answers. Maybe trying to solve the universe like a puzzle was missing the point of existence in the first place.

Figuring everything out was lonely and unsatisfying, but experiencing the many complexities of life with a contemplative and open mind gave me access not only to other people, but to a deeper understanding of myself.

As a bonus, I also realized how silly my confidence in being right had been in the first place. Lots of humans a lot smarter than me have been wrong about a lot of things, so how could I be sure I was right about anything?

I decided to enjoy the conversation, to be curious about other people's opinions, and to seek to understand rather than to be understood.

Once I did, I found satisfaction. I still had deep thoughts. I still examined the world around me. But I appreciated mystery and enigma. I didn't feel like I had to figure everything out, and I didn't feel like I had to tell everybody else what I knew.

In your life, I think you'll find that questions are more valuable than the answers. I think you'll find dialog more interesting than debate. I think you'll discover that curiosity is honest, and that certainty is fraud.

I want you to embrace the mysteries of life and to be humble. Do that, and you'll find deeper thoughts than you imagined possible.

Don't let best prevent better

There is an old parable I learned as a kid that I've never forgotten.

When God was creating the world, He lined up all the birds to give them their feathers. As each bird stepped to the front of the line, God reached into His trunk and offered the animal a set of feathers, which they could accept and wear, or reject and get back in line to try again.

A particular bird came near to the front of the line and watched as one bird became the blue jay and another became the cardinal. He could barely contain his excitement as the bird in front of him became the bald eagle. He wondered what majestic set of feathers God would offer him as he stepped to the front.

When God pulled from the trunk the bright coat of the toucan, the bird was dazzled. He imagined himself with a long beak and pleasant colors admired by people all over the world. He knew he would be happy as a toucan, but might always wonder what he could have been if only he had waited for something better.

The bird declined God's offer and instead got back in line to try again.

The bird watched in awe as God revealed flamingos, penguins, and owls from the trunk. He shook with anticipation as he again came to the front, and God reached deep down to pull up his next option. This time, God offered him the feathers of the peregrine falcon, sharp and swift. The bird beamed at the thought of being the world's fastest animal and nearly pounced on the impressive design. But once more, he hesitated, wondering whether, if he passed up this offer, perfection itself would yet lay ahead.

Again the bird declined and returned to the back of the line.

But this time, the bird watched with dismay as it took longer and longer for God to retrieve the feathery suits in the depths of the trunk. The colors seemed less bright, the abilities less impressive. When finally the bird came to the front of the line, God spent what seemed like an eternity searching the trunk for anything still remaining.

As it turned out, there was only one left. God handed it to him, and he felt shabby and disheveled as he put on his robe. His head was naked and unfeathered, his beak sharp and sloped, his eyes dark and scowling, his legs unadorned and drab. Neither designed for beauty nor speed, this suit of feathers he now wore was the envy of none: he had become the vulture.

As the vulture looked into the mirror he realized that he was destined to be the symbol of death, unadmired and dreaded all his days. At that moment, he longed to be the impressive falcon or the delightful toucan, but because he so valued perfection, he had failed to accept the better feathers God had offered him.

We, like the vulture, are also prone to passing up improvement because it is imperfect. But success is incremental, and perfection doesn't exist.

In your life, be careful not to pass up on *better* in your pursuit of *best*. The ideal job, the ideal mate, the ideal home, the ideal life may never present itself. If you keep passing better options, you may be disappointed in what you're left with at the end.

Cut your own meat

When you were little, you'd occasionally swap the grilled cheese on the kids' menu for a steak or chicken breast.

However, as refined as your tastes had become, you were still powerless to enjoy your meal unless I grabbed the knife and fork and diced everything up for you. Your ignorance of how to use the tools on the dinner table limited your ability to eat.

The same is often true in your career. You are only as powerful as your knowledge of how things work. If other people have information that you don't, then you are dependent on them.

This is why you should gladly assist in—or even do—the work of your colleagues. Happily have them show you what they do and offer to take care of that for them in the future.

Seize their treasure of information and unlock each new task and system. Reveal the secrets of their skills and, eventually, you will be more valuable than they are.

Do not resent your co-workers or your leaders when they ask you to do their work. The fools are *giving* away their power, and you should hungrily take it.

Once you know how to cut your own meat, you won't be dependent on others to eat.

Speak from the heart

Smart people often get frustrated that others don't listen to them.

It can feel like people ignore your advice, and you can find yourself discouraged that your best ideas fall upon deaf ears.

Always begin your speaking with listening. Absorb what others are feeling and reflect that back to them.

Tell them how you feel about them, or why you desire to help them. Make them understand the human connection that you have to their situation. Then offer advice.

Nobody cares how much you know until they know how much you care.

Be slow to boil

In sophomore chemistry class, I learned that water has a property called "specific heat".

At first, I thought it would be a good name for a rock band, but, as I discovered, it means that it takes a lot of energy to raise the temperature of water even one degree. A lot more than other chemicals, anyway.

I remember being impressed. I imagined all the heat a flame is pouring into water, and the H2O just taking it like a champ, until it begrudgingly ticks up a notch on the thermometer. It made me respect the power of a cool bottle of water on a hot summer day.

I think the best people I know have that property as well. They can be in hot situations with fiery people and keep their cool.

Anger is stupid and self-defeating. Angry people almost never get what they want. Calm people usually do.

I think of anger as a weakness, a low boiling point which limits how useful you are in the real world.

We think we have the right to be angry, that others *made* us this way. We feel entitled to it. But anger is nothing more than self-indulgent surrender.

It is a relief to get angry, to tell others how angry we are. It allows us to abandon the slow and tedious work of solving problems.

You'll find that you're much more successful when you absorb the anger of others without becoming angry yourself. Stay cool, and you'll be fine.

Don't look at the egg

When something is really important, we become afraid of losing it. Sometimes this fear causes us to sabotage ourselves, and we end up losing it anyway.

Ironically, the only way I know to ensure that you don't lose something that is important to you is to look beyond it, to avoid overvaluing it, and to imagine that it isn't really there at all.

There is a game that illustrates my point: You give kids a spoon, place an egg on the spoon, and have them race one another. Drop the egg, you lose. Finish the race, you win.

Inevitably, each kid does the same thing. They stare at the egg balanced precariously at the end of their outstretched arm and gingerly pace forward. Their arms sway, their grip tightens, they panic, and before long, down goes Humpty Dumpty.

The trick to winning this game is to look past the egg toward the finish line. Do that, and your grip remains firm, your arm will be steady, and your momentum will correct any wobbling until you reach the end.

The same is true in life. If you become too focused on something you're afraid of losing—a job, a relationship, an achievement—you will likely lose it as a result of your attention. Keep it in your peripheral vision, and focus on where you're going, not on what you're afraid of dropping.

Life is fair

When you were in the single-digit years, you discovered the word "fair", and it almost ruined my life.

It's hard to be lectured by a kid about the vast and complicated nuances of social justice every time they aren't offered dessert or don't get a toy at the store, or you slay them in a video game their mother doesn't know you're letting them play.

You'd scream and roll on the floor anytime anything didn't go your way, usually pointing out that it wasn't "fair". Typically, a grown-up response to that is, "Life isn't fair." But I never said that to you, because I don't believe it's true.

Life *is* fair, because life is *random*.

Steve Jobs, the guy who founded Apple, Inc., was the richest man on Earth when he died young of pancreatic cancer. If life wasn't fair, rich people like him could stave off death no matter the problem. But life is fair, because even a billionaire with everything going for him can die from something that is equally likely to kill anybody else.

Manhattan is equally likely to be obliterated by an asteroid as Bangladesh, a lottery winner has the same odds as all the lottery losers, and every single living thing on the planet got here because of trillions of random coincidences.

Random, to me, means that "all options are possible". And because we all have that in common, life is actually quite fair.

I realize that all things aren't equal. I realize that injustice exists. I realize that lots of people have more than they deserve, and lots of other people have less than they are owed.

But as a dad, I want you to be the best version of yourself and to utilize the resources you have. I don't want you to be paralyzed by envy or distracted by the advantages of others.

Accepting that life is random, and, therefore, fair, frees you of all the foot stomping and breath holding.

Accepting that makes you take charge of your life and look for opportunities to improve your odds.

Accepting that takes away the pouting and the victim thinking.

So do what you can with what you've got, because life is as fair as it's going to get.

Take your feelings to court

It's normal to have anxiety or to get depressed. It's normal to compare yourself to other people, and it's normal to suspect that many are doing better than you.

It's normal to worry about the future, to experience hopelessness, or to be overcome with rage.

Emotions are—probably—what make us human. They aren't bad. They aren't good. They just are. It's important to identify them when they happen rather than to pretend that you don't have them at all.

But it's also important to distrust them.

When you feel something, it's tempting to believe it. I *feel* scared, so there must be something to fear. I *feel* rejected, so I must be unlovable. I *feel* angry, so anger will probably help me solve my problem.

But feelings aren't facts.

They are a reflexive reaction to what life appears to be, not a thoughtful response to the way things actually are.

I've known so many people who allow their feelings to determine their actions, people who view the world through emotional lenses and believe what they see. But if you live your life in this way, you'll find that, nine in ten times, you bump your head on avoidable obstacles or make things worse altogether.

Before you take action in life, pause and reflect on what you think you see. Imagine yourself putting your feelings on trial with an especially cranky judge on the bench. Present your case for the feeling being true, and attempt to prove beyond a shadow of a doubt that your emotion is right, and that the situation is guilty.

Keep in mind the judge has a duty to presume innocence, and that you'll need more than hearsay, suspicion, or assumption to get a verdict. Once you've presented the case, take the opposite side, listing all the reasons that your emotion could be coming to the wrong conclusion. Stick to evidence only—just the facts—and see if that helps you figure out the truth behind your feeling.

Whatever you do in the end, be wary of emotional conclusions. Feelings aren't facts.

Don't tailgate your heart

I realize I can come off as a cynic. I know you hesitate before you tell me about your hopes and ideas because you're afraid I'll crap all over them.

That's fair.

But maybe you'd be surprised to learn that I DO want you to be guided by your passions. I DO want you to set big, audacious goals, and I DO want you to imagine and to try.

I just don't want you to set your sights so far down the road that you plow into the flashing brake lights of reality.

Go for it in life, take chances and make mistakes. Just give yourself enough room to fail.

Follow your heart, but don't tailgate.

Patience is a choice

It drives me nuts when people say that they ran out of patience, or that they snapped because an unlikely series of events occurred that gives them permission to self-destruct or to ruin the lives of others.

That's not how it works.

Patience is not a limited resource, something you can run out of or run low on. Patience is an inexhaustible choice, an action that you can do an infinite number of times, until you choose to stop doing it.

Patience is a choice, not a commodity.

When you are stressed, don't indulge in the fantasy that you have permission to lose your cool. Some of the worst decisions are preceded by an announcement that the decider is "out of patience". There is no such thing. What they are really saying is that they have reached the end of their ability to lead and are prepared to be unwise to soothe their own irritation.

Choose patience.

Don't trade reals for ideals

If history had a cemetery, it would be loaded with the bodies of idiots who gave up their lives for some invisible set of ideas. Fools who traded the here and now—their families, communities and a lifetime of stories—in the name of pride, principles, or philosophies.

We write about people like that and tell you to idolize them. We do that to build character during your formative years, but when you become an adult, you'll need to abandon that hocus pocus and open your eyes.

I've seen lots of know-it-all, self-righteous martyrs trade real things in life, because they believe that justice, honor, or some other virtue demands it. They've quit their jobs, passed up opportunities, or even traded their relationships in the name of some intangible rule or idea.

I'm a pragmatic guy, and I'll be disappointed if I see you waving zeal and ideas around like a flag, decrying the messy inconsistency of life and abandoning your commitments.

There is a time and place for that sort of inflexible idealism, to be sure. But in your day-to-day life, you're going to have ample opportunities to assert that some invisible principle must be honored, and that your marriage or job or friendship must be sacrificed on an altar to appease it.

There is no honor for the fools who traded away what they have to satisfy an idea. You can't hold honor in your arms. You can't kiss justice. Value the tangible treasures in your life.

If you have to choose between being happy and being right, choose happy.

Trust interest, not loyalty

Your grandfather says that everybody's favorite radio station is WIIFM: What's In It For Me? If you aren't broadcasting on that frequency, they won't stay tuned for long.

I think he's right. When we are bringing friends and family aboard new projects, we tend to assume they will align with our best interests out of loyalty or dependability. That isn't how life works, though.

When you have skin in the game, you want the people on your team to have an interest in winning, not merely in saving your skin. They must have something worth getting for themselves, something that will motivate them and give them an inward desire to succeed.

Be wary of trusting people in life who express loyalty to you, but who don't appear to have an interest of their own. They may be sincere and genuine, but only self-interest is reliable when times get tough.

Let go of monkey traps

Baboons are terrifying.

Routinely they are beefed up to 100 pounds, as jacked as bodybuilders and with teeth like daggers, able to crush your bones in a single bite. None of this would be alarming if the little demons didn't also belong to troops of 50 monkies or more with the emotional temperament of toddlers.

Basically, if you see one, you're supposed to run away and pee on yourself to show submission.

I may have made up the pee part.

In Africa, when a hunter wants to trap a baboon, he has to outsmart it.

First, he gets something that looks valuable—a watch, seeds, Honus Wagner baseball card—whatever, just as long as the baboon sees him holding the thing, and he pretends that it's important.

Second, he digs a hole in hard earth (clay, rock, or a termite mound) and places the bait in the hole. Then he walks away.

The baboon's curiosity will eventually overtake him, and he will march over to the hole, slip in his hand through the narrow tunnel, make a fist around the thing he saw put in there, and try to get it out. But his clenched fist won't fit back through the tunnel. He'll be stuck.

At this point the hunter strolls out, whistling a jaunty tune and swinging a machete. The baboon howls in terror, and his body flails wildly as he tries to escape his demise.

At any moment the baboon could release the treasure and slip his hand back out—but he won't. His closed fist refuses to release the thing in the hole, and so he is trapped under his own power.

He will die, because he can't let go.

Humans can be just the same. Because we can't let go of something, we often fall into traps that will lead to our own downfall.

When we are offended, we can't let it go.

When we have been let down, we can't let it go.

When we are resentful, we can't let it go.

When we have an impossible dream, and we can't let it go.

When people keep hurting us, but we can't let them go.

Just like the baboon, if you don't let things go, you'll be trapped. Ironically, nothing whatsoever is keeping you trapped except yourself.

You only need to let it go.

Step into the pitch

When you were little, you were afraid of playing catch.

I tried to teach you to keep your eye on the ball, but even when I floated it gently toward you, instead of snagging it with your baseball glove, you'd wretch away like it was a hornet.

Your fear of the ball was insurmountable. I tried encouraging you, reminding you, even drawing a happy face on the ball; nothing worked.

Finally, I just pitched one right into your chest. It landed with a thud and dropped to the ground in front of you. It happened too fast for you to wince or react. You just stared down at the motionless baseball for several seconds.

You looked up with a smile, surprised that it didn't hurt as much as you thought. You were startled, but fine. You picked up the ball and threw it back.

You've been playing catch ever since.

In life, you are going to fear some things. Often, your fear is way bigger than the power or pain of the thing itself. Unfortunately, you won't be very comforted when people tell you this, or when you try to say it to yourself, so your best option is to step into the pitch.

Let the ball hit you. Stand up to exactly the thing you're afraid of.

Do that, and you'll find that your fear is much more painful than the thing itself. Its sting will teach you that you are bigger and more resilient than you think you are.

Don't be afraid of the ball.

Don't follow your dreams

You're going to see a lot of posters on walls in school that talk about doing what you're passionate about and daring to dream big. I'm fine with that.

But it's foolish to spend your whole life chasing the wind. Dreams are, by definition, the opposite of reality; they are illusions that only work when you're sleeping.

They don't have to make sense. They don't have to be probable. They don't have to live up to the hype.

I've met plenty of idiots who have a dream. Since the invention of the internet, it seems that there is no shortage of morons who want to be famous for something or rich for no reason. They want to sing a pop song or perform a stunt or be handed an advertising deal for being a conspicuously obnoxious and unforgettable spectacle.

I don't want that for you. Even if they achieve their dreams, most people find nothing but emptiness on the other side.

That's because after you dream, you wake up.

I'd rather you follow your *aspirations*. Aspire to live a satisfying life. A life filled with stories and fulfilled goals. A real life. Not a dream one.

Be realistic, and don't cry about it. Don't sob in the corner about how, your whole life, you've only wanted one thing, and I'm cynically telling you not to do it.

If you've spent your whole life wanting only one thing, I pity you. You haven't lived. You've only dreamed.

Let pain teach you

Part of being alive is feeling pain. The only pain-free humans are dead.

Discomfort. Loss. Sorrow. Embarrassment. Grief. Envy. All of it is part of living.

Pain has a purpose. It's the simplest and most-powerful-of-all education. You do something. It hurts. You don't do it again.

When you were little, I tried to keep you from hurting yourself. I got really anxious about it, if you want to know the truth. I'd freak out when you were hurt and hate myself for not protecting you.

I'd wince whenever you were jumping on the couch or pushing back in the chair at the kitchen table, remembering when I've gotten hurt doing the same things, and wanting to reach out and stop you.

But then I realized that, if I stopped you, if I saved you, you'd never wince at danger like I do.

Pain can teach you, if you're willing to learn from it.

When pain happens, people will try to comfort you, to console you. You'll want them to, and that's fine. But don't let the pain fade away into memory without taking a lesson from it, and don't be surprised if you have to get hurt lots of times before you figure it out.

A man once wrote, "There are an infinity of angles at which men fall, but only one at which they stand."

That's a clever way of saying that, sometimes, there is one right way to do something, and you probably won't know what that is until you fail a few dozen times.

Beware the sorrow of cheat codes

My generation invented video games.

Wait—the one before me did, I think.

My generation *played* video games.

During the era of my youth, it was common for kids to discover "cheat codes" for these games. Developers would embed all sorts of shortcuts and power-ups that would give the player god-like abilities. The hardest levels would be skipped over on a whim, and the toughest bosses would be slain beneath the devastating might of invincibility and infinite ammo.

Using these codes, my friends and I were drunk with power, taking turns beating the game and relishing the sweet vengeance of dancing on the graves of our 8-bit enemies.

But then we were bored. Worse than that, somehow, using the cheat codes took away the fun of the game entirely.

Why do the hard work of mastering the skills needed to win the game, of exploring the worlds or solving the puzzles, when, at any time, you can just smash a few buttons and win? It wasn't fun anymore. Winning became hollow and pointless.

I think this can be true in real life too. If we allow ourselves to think that the point of life is merely to win (whatever that means), then we can wish for the fast-track, instant paths to winning. But when you look at the people who have had that, they don't look happy.

Once they have it all, there is nothing left. They skipped the story, the adventure, the point. They traded the game itself for the end credits and high score, never really knowing if the game was fun at all.

A man once told me, "The reward for a job well done is to have done it." His point was that if we focus only on the finish line, we will forget the fun of running the race.

In your life, I hope you won't focus so much on the end-game that you forget the game itself. I also hope you don't use cheat codes. I hope you don't look for shortcuts and hacks that take away the frustratingly slow, yet surprisingly satisfying crawl of reality.

Because I want you to be happy, and we are happiest when we are playing the game, not when we've won it.

Don't apologize for the rain

You're a nice person. I like that about you. I raised you to say you're sorry when you screw up and to make amends whenever possible.

But don't spend any good minutes of our short lives angsting over the displeasure that others experience which you didn't cause.

You can't own things outside your control. It's natural to feel badly about other people's problems, but you have to be careful not to attach too much, or accept responsibility for solving them.

Maybe people want to blame you. Fine. That'll happen. Sometimes you can help them see it's not your fault, and sometimes you can't. In the meantime, don't emotionally own any of it.

If you personalize the problems or misfortunes of others you will live a life of misery and anxiety.

You're not secretly God, you are not somehow connected to or responsible for everybody's troubles.

Unless you are secretly God, in which case thanks for the Cubs winning the 2016 World Series.

Love conditionally

At some point movies and television gave people the idea that *real* love is something we give to another person regardless of how they treat us. Unconditional love no matter what.

That's wrong. You shouldn't love people unconditionally. Because you can't.

Let me explain what I mean by "love", I think there are two types: First, the verb "love", which is doing kindness, affection and loyalty at somebody. Second, the noun "love", which describes a feeling we have.

To me the verb and noun are two sides of the same coin. You can't *do* love authentically if you don't *feel* love genuinely.

Unlike actions, feelings are conditional. You can promise, unconditionally, to stop at red lights even if you're in a hurry. You can't promise to never feel impatient.

This is where love is different from other actions and other feelings. It's not possible to promise to feel a certain way about a person forever, so it's not possible to behave as if you did feel that way forever either.

That doesn't mean you can't be polite, or treat people with kindness and respect. It doesn't mean you abandon people and give up on them merely because you aren't feeling them at the moment. You can still commit to people and be loyal to them without loving them.

But, the truth is that our ability to feel love for people is dependent on those people's ability to be lovable, which can change. It means that love - whether you like it or not - is conditional.

As it should be.

When humans get a guarantee without requirements they take it for granted. They stop being grateful and they stop trying to be worthy. They become toxically selfish and blind to the needs of others.

In your life I want you to value love. I want you to see the love you give to others as something worth trying for. I want you to see the love you get from others as something worth earning. I want you to love genuinely and not out of obligation. I also want you to see the importance of being a lovable person.

Love is something people must maintain, not something they are entitled to.

Do the next right thing

Lots of people are bad at making decisions. That's because they think of too much at once.

Whatever you're facing, whatever the risks, whatever the nuances and obstacles and dangers, do only the next right thing. Take a second to imagine what that might be.

Do that.

Then what?

Do the next right thing.

Then what?

Do the next right thing.

Keep it simple. You'll be fine.

Get action

Theodore Roosevelt embodied ambition.

He was the President of the United States. He was also the Vice President, the Governor of New York, the Secretary of the Navy, the Police Commissioner of New York City, a Captain in the Army (won a Medal of Honor), a Nobel Peace Prize recipient, a state assemblyman, and a cowboy in the wild west.

A freaking cowboy! Look it up.

While Roosevelt was campaigning for the presidency, a man shot him *in the chest*. Refusing to go to the hospital, Teddy instead gave a 90-minute speech that began with, "Ladies and gentlemen, I don't know whether you understand that I have just been shot, but it takes more than that to kill a bull-moose."

Roosevelt chopped his own wood while in the White House. He read thousands of books in multiple languages. He boxed professional opponents (was even blinded in his left eye *while President*). He was an avid hunter, horseback rider, tennis player, boat rower, and had a third-degree brown belt in judo.

In the winter, Theodore Roosevelt would skinny dip in the Potomac River—to relax.

But in his early years, Roosevelt embodied frailty. He was bedridden and sickly. He couldn't go outside. He couldn't leave his room. He wasn't even allowed to open the windows.

He even survived personal tragedy: the death of his mother (typhoid) and his wife (kidney failure) in the same house, within a day of each other.

Through unimaginable hardship and mental anguish, Theodore Roosevelt overcame everything to become one of the most admired Presidents of all time, and he did it all simply by believing that he could handle more, and then proving himself right.

He adhered to a philosophy he called "get action". Basically, he believed that the best life worth living was the one where he could have as many adventures as possible. He liked challenges. He liked hardship. It excited him.

Too often in life we throw our hands up and say, "I can't." We give in and feel sorry for ourselves.

Instead, we should *run toward* our challenges.

Tell yourself that you are stronger than you appear.

Tell yourself that you are eager to have an adventure. Shake yourself out of fear and plunge into the problem.

To get through it, get action.

Sit on your hands

A pilot once told me a story about how he escaped imminent death by doing nothing, and it's since become my mantra for dealing with crises.

As the story goes he was flying over the Gulf of Mexico one dark and cloudy night when his plane engines died.

Now if you've ever ridden in an airplane, you know the sound of those engines. They roar to life when you take off, and you can't hear the snoring of the person next to you until you land. Imagine being six miles up in a pitch-black sky when, suddenly, that soothing whir of jets spitting out thrust turns into deafening silence.

Now imagine the feeling of your seat belt pulling down on your waist as the plane falls from the sky.

The pilot searched his dashboard desperately as his passengers began screaming in terror, every passing moment hastening his plummet toward the sea. But instead of reacting to the fear, instead of springing into action by turning knobs and flipping switches in a frenzied attempt to rescue himself from doom, he steadied himself and did something I never would have guessed.

He sat on his hands.

He told me that pilots are trained to understand that the most dangerous threat to the aircraft is not the turbulence of the sky, or the lightning in the clouds, or even gravity's irresistible fist.

The most dangerous threat to the airplane is the pilot.

He sat on his hands to prevent himself from letting trouble become tragedy. He knew that if he began wildly turning dials, he might actually make the situation worse. So he sat on his hands and thought through the problem.

It's hard to think clearly when your bag of pretzels is floating up near your nose, but by slowing himself down, he was able to identify the problem and plan a solution. He finally removed a hand from beneath him and tried a series of switch flips and button pushes, being careful to get each action correct despite the ear-piercing screams he heard through his cockpit door.

The engine came alive. He brought the plane out of its dive and regained control.

In your life, you will experience terrifying situations. You will feel desperate, out of control, and you will be tempted to respond fast by going with the first thing that pops into your mind. Your hands will metaphorically be flipping switches and turning knobs in wild desperation to solve the problem.

Don't do that. The most dangerous person in your life is *you*. Not other people, not numbers in a bank account, not health test results—*you*.

When you are in peril the most intelligent thing you can do is *nothing*. Sit on your hands and stop yourself from making the problem worse than it already is. Approach it with a clear mind and take deliberate actions to solve it.

Never underestimate your ability to turn trouble into tragedy.

Name your problem

We all have problems.

Maybe you want to lose some weight, lower your anxiety, climb out of depression, or just overcome your procrastination. You may even be discouraged because you've tried and failed to fix those problems.

Part of the reason we fail is because we are thinking about the problem in the wrong way.

We talk about problems as if they are part of us: "I am depressed", "I am anxious", "I procrastinate", "I can't stop eating," and so on. That's called "internalization". We are internalizing the problem, not knowing where it ends and we begin.

It's pretty hard to deny myself a slice of red velvet cake. It's about as effective as handcuffing myself to the gate when I have the keys in my pocket.

You can't beat the problem if you are the problem.

A better way is to describe the problem as outside of yourself, which is called "externalization". Describe the problem as if it were a being with a personality, a desire, an agenda, and even a face. Answer questions like, "What does it want?", and "How does it trick me?"

The power of your mind is unlocked when it has an imaginary opponent to face off against, instead of just trying to deal with itself. It's hard to tell *myself* not to feel anxious when I have a meeting with my boss tomorrow morning; it's a little easier to defy Nervous Nancy, the imaginary, shaking lady who is furiously biting her nails and telling me to panic all the time.

Name your bad habits. Describe them as a person. Draw them. Start referring to them by name with others. Defy them and draw out a plan to prevent them from winning.

Top off the bottle

I really like those old glass Coke bottles, the eight-ounce ones that fit right in your hand and make a great foghorn sound when you blow across the top. I used to keep one in my car, so that I could twirl it around while I drove, sort of my version of a stress ball.

From time to time, I also use that empty Coke bottle to teach people a lesson about getting a problem out of their lives.

First I present the bottle to a group of people, along with a basket of random office supplies (paper clips, rubber bands, pens, sticky notes, etc.). Then I pull the cap off a typical plastic ballpoint pen and plop it into the empty Coke bottle. I give the people five minutes to get the pen cap out of the bottle using the supplies, but they aren't allowed to break the bottle or touch it with their creations in any way whatsoever.

After a while I come back to see that people have made all sorts of impressive retrieving devices, but try as they might, nobody ever succeeds without cheating.

I compare the activity to the way people come up with all sorts of elaborate ways to remove a problem from their life. They cobble together various tools to get the problem out without destroying themselves, but, often, the process just becomes frustrating and unsuccessful.

So how do you get the pen cap out?

I usually place a cup of some kind next to the basket of supplies. People assume it's my own water cup, so they politely don't touch it; but in reality, it was always part of the game. I pick up the cup and pour the water into the Coke bottle. The pen cap floats up to the neck, then to the mouth, and if you top off the bottle, the pen cap will bob up over the rim and present itself to be plucked.

I explain that the best way to remove a problem from your life is to fill your time with something nourishing. Water is necessary for life, so it's a great metaphor. If you want to get rid of something fill the empty space with something better; eventually, the good will push out the bad, and you won't have the problem inside anymore.

That's something I want you to know as well. There will be times in your life when you are bedeviled by a problem that won't go away, maybe a toxic relationship or a bad habit, and the best way I know to get rid of that thing is to fill your life with *more*, until there is very little room left for the problem.

Don't have to

When I was younger, every second of my life was stressful.

By day, I was a high school history teacher; by night, I worked for free at a therapy clinic as an intern; and by late night, I did my homework for my graduate school classes. When I wasn't doing those things, I had a wife complaining that I was never around, a kid who needed me, a mortgage to pay, broken cars to fix, and overdue bills stacked on the kitchen table.

I was miserable.

One night I got home after a long, 14-hour day that had stressed me to my breaking point. I walked into the empty living room and heard your mom bathing you upstairs. Hoping you didn't hear me and subsequently summon me to play with you, I tiptoed into the kitchen to find my dinner waiting for me on the stove, cold.

"What a life," I thought. "I have to work all day, I have to work all night, I have to come home to cold dinner, and I'll probably have to go upstairs and entertain my kid. Then I'll have to talk to my wife and hear about her day before I come downstairs and eat dinner alone in front of the TV."

Just then, our new puppy looked up at me with those big brown eyes, and peed all over the kitchen floor.

Red-faced, I gritted my teeth and balled my fists. I swore in whispers as I ripped sheets of paper towels and knelt down to the kitchen floor. I was seconds away from screaming in anger or collapsing in tears.

But I'll never forget the moment I pressed that wad of paper towels down on the linoleum floor. As I felt that warm puppy pee against the palm of my hand, I experienced something like an epiphany. Kneeling on the floor in my uncomfortable dress shirt and slacks, I realized something that would change my life forever.

I don't *have* to. I *get* to.

I *get* to have a job as a teacher. I *get* to work at a clinic helping people in the evenings. I *get* to come home and play with *my* child, who actually wants to see me. I *get* to talk to *my* wife, who wants to share her life with me. I *get* to watch television and eat reheated food made for me.

I *get* to clean up *my* puppy's pee.

You've probably heard that beauty is in the eye of the beholder. So is happiness. So much of our lives are spent resenting and keeping score, adding up all the injustices and inadequacies, wishing that life would just cut us some slack. But you'll be amazed how your world changes if you just change the way you speak about it. If you just change the way you think about it.

You don't *have* to. You *get* to.

Say that to yourself for an entire week. Every time you get called into a meeting. Every time you have a new assignment thrust into your lap. Every time your dog pees on the floor.

Life is a privilege, not an obligation. Happiness is a choice. We begin to live into that choice when we change our vocabulary, when we change the thoughts we think and the words we say.

Don't have to—*get* to.

Epilogue

I love you.

I'm *so* proud of you.

I know I must have made a million mistakes. I know you resent me for some of those.

Please, forgive me.

If I ever made you feel less than wonderful, forgive me.

If I ever scared you or made you feel unsafe, forgive me.

If I ever ignored you, abandoned you, or left you waiting, forgive me.

I don't ask your forgiveness for my sake, but for your own. So you can have peace.

As your father, I have an undeserved amount of influence in your heart. I'd be dangerous with even a tenth of that power, and I'm not qualified to have even a hundredth of it.

There are no awards for giving fatherhood a shot. We mostly get remembered for the few times we dropped you and not the thousands we lifted you up on our shoulders.

But I get it. I had a dad too.

You and I are bonded by some mysterious and powerful force. We are connected through space and time, and even though I may not be with you, my words will live on forever inside of you. That's just the way it is, whether those words were good or bad.

That's why I wrote you this book.

I hope that these words comfort you. I hope that they remind you of the goodness I see in you. I hope that they whisper to you in the darkest nights of your life and give you peace.

I hope that my words calm you as they did when you were a baby crying on my shoulder.

I hope that, somehow, they are louder than the words I said that hurt you. I hope that these better words endure.

You're going to be okay.

I know that because you're strong, you're good, and you're kind.

You're going to be okay.

I know that because there isn't anything you aren't capable of. You've done a million things that have blown my mind, and I have unshakable confidence in your ability to adapt and to thrive.

You're going to be okay.

I know that because I've seen this world and the people in it. Things might scare us, but everything usually turns out alright.

You're going to be ok.

Love,

Dad

About the Author

Dr. Jim Jobin is a psychotherapist who has spent tens of thousands of hours helping his patients navigate the complexities of life and manage their mental health. He is known as much for his down to Earth approach and disarming humor as his pragmatic solution focused coaching style. Jim has served as President of both the Nevada Counseling Association and the National Alliance on Mental Illness Southern Nevada, has been honored at the Governor's Point of Light Awards, and has been appointed to multiple terms of service on the Southern Nevada Behavioral Health Policy and Advisory Board.

To learn more about Dr. Jim Jobin, follow him on social media or request a speaking engagement please visit **www.DadviceBook.com**

www.ingramcontent.com/pod-product-compliance
Lightning Source LLC
Chambersburg PA
CBHW030328160726
47992CB00005B/2207